I0760063

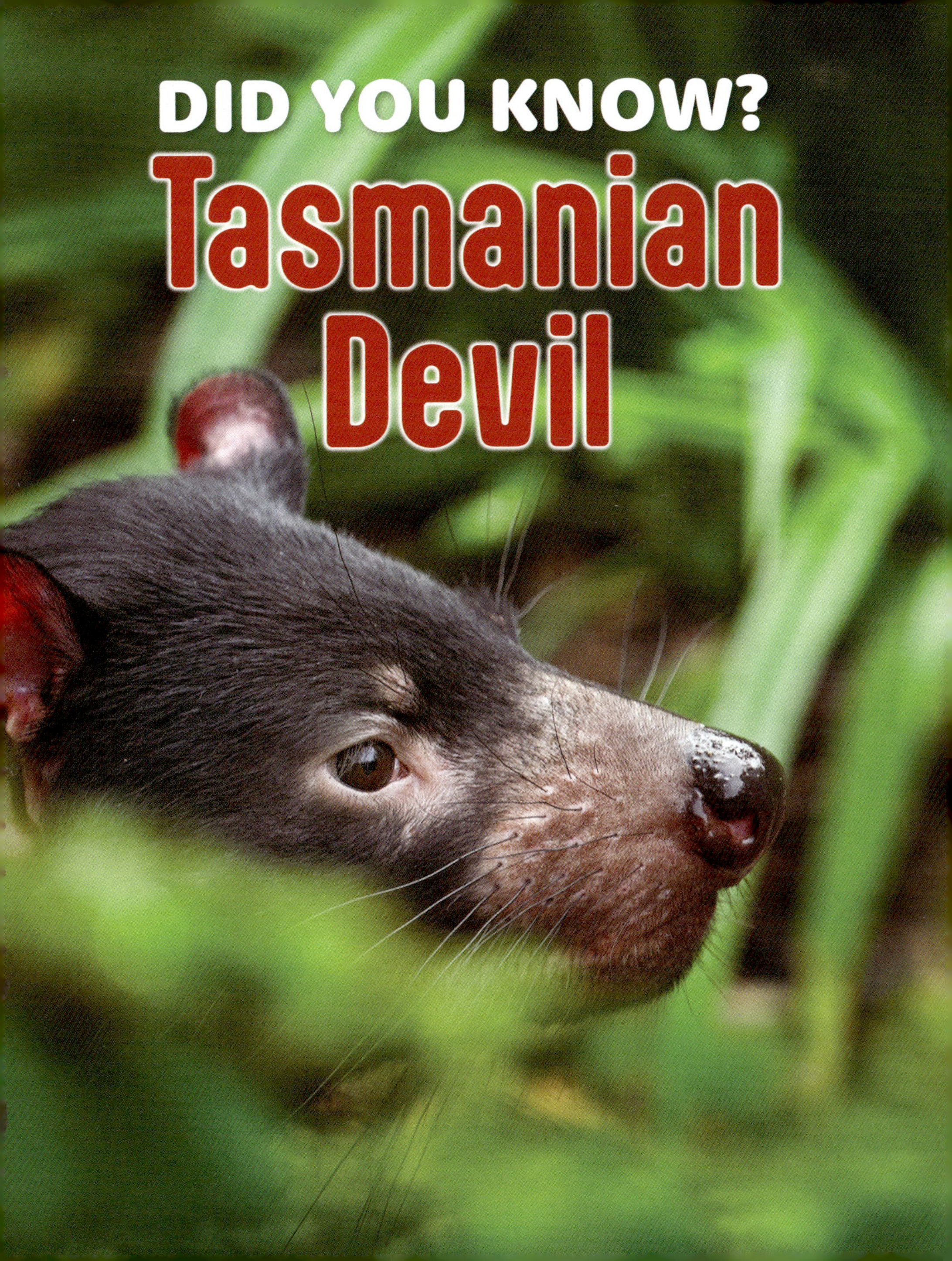
DID YOU KNOW?
Tasmanian
Devil

DID YOU KNOW?

Tasmanian Devil

Contents

What is a Tasmanian Devil?

● Tasmanian Devils are **mammals** belonging to the **marsupial** family, alongside the likes of kangaroos and wombats. Mammals are covered in fur and babies feed on their mother's **milk**, while the young of marsupials develop in mum's **pouch**.

- Devils have short **blackish fur**, often with a **white patch** on the chest, rounded ears, short legs and a long, thin tail.
- **Unlike** most of their marsupial relatives, Tasmanian Devils feed on **meat.**
- They tend to be **solitary** – living and hunting **alone**, except when a female is looking after her young for the first few months of life.

Facts and figures

- Tasmanian Devils grow to about **seventy centimetres** long and can weigh up to **ten kilograms**. When fully grown they can be similar in length and weight to a **medium-sized dog**.
- There may be as few as **twenty thousand** adult devils surviving in the wild – that's barely enough to fill the Bellerive Oval **sports stadium** in the Tasmanian city of Hobart!
- Despite their small legs, devils can run at speeds of more than **twenty kilometres** per hour for short bursts.

Special adaptations

- The Tasmanian Devil has the **strongest bite** of any animal of its size – it can bite through bone and even metal wire. Its long **canine teeth** are ideal for eating meat.
- Devils are **nocturnal** hunters, meaning that they are mostly active at **night**. They are also **crepuscular**, often going about their business at **dawn** and **dusk**.
- During the **daytime** they usually rest in dense bush or in a **hollow trunk** or hole in the ground.
- It may seem surprising, but devils can **climb high** into trees, and they are also strong **swimmers**.

Where do they live?

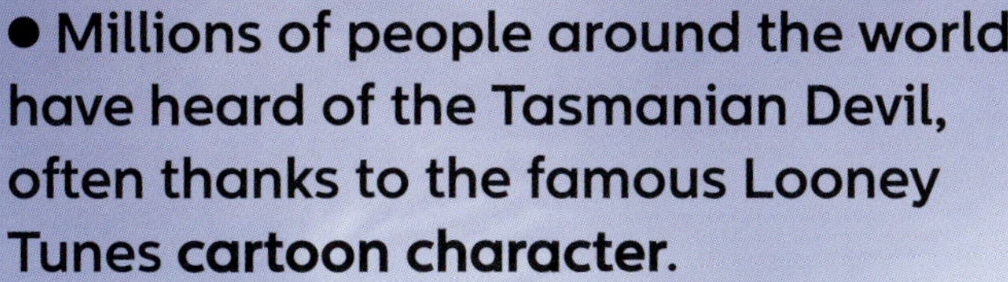

- Millions of people around the world have heard of the Tasmanian Devil, often thanks to the famous Looney Tunes **cartoon character**.

- Real-life Tasmanian Devils are kept in **zoos** and **animal parks** around the world, where they have become a favourite attraction for millions of people.

- In the wild, however, devils live only on their namesake Australian island of **Tasmania**, where they can be found a variety of habitats, including **forests**, **woodlands** and areas of **scrub**.

Closest relatives

- Famously, today the Tasmanian Devil is known as the world's **largest carnivorous marsupial.**

Tasmanian Devil.

- However, that title used to belong to the now-extinct **Thylacine** – or 'Tasmanian Tiger' – which had a body measuring more than **one metre** in length. Thylacines shared the island of Tasmania with the devils and would have been a predator of the smaller animals.
- The devil's closest living relatives include other meat-eating members of the same family – such as the various species of **quoll** found on Tasmania and the Australian mainland.

Quoll – you can see the resemblance to a devil.

Thylacine.

Image: Harry Burrell © Public Domain

What's for dinner?

- Tasmanian Devils are **carnivores** – they eat mostly meat, so they catch other animals and feed on them.
- Devils can catch and eat prey as large as a wallaby or small kangaroo.

- They are also scavengers, feeding on dead animals. This food source is known as carrion. Often dead animals make up more of a devil's diet than live prey.
- Insects, birds, reptiles, frogs, fish and sometimes plants are also eaten.

Family life

- As with other marsupials, young devils are born small – about the size of a single **grain of rice** – and in a litter of up to **forty** babies. At this stage the young are known as **imps**.

- The imps crawl to their mother's **pouch**. She has only four teats so only the quickest few imps will survive – it is literally a **race for life**.
- Just like kangaroos, larger baby Tasmanian Devils are called **joeys**.
- Joeys stay in the pouch for four months and continue to feed on their **mum's milk** for the first ten months of life.

Two joeys playing.

Are they rare?

- Tasmanian Devils are considered to be an **endangered species.**
- Many of the major threats to devils are due to the activities of **humans**, such as **deforestation** and destroying their habitat in other ways to make way for buildings and farmland.

Road sign warning drivers to watch out for devils.

- Adult devils have no natural native predators, although Wedge-tailed Eagles and predators introduced by humans – such as **foxes** – can kill the young.

- Other potential problems include **climate change** affecting their habitat and food supply, or **road-traffic collisions** killing devils.

Red Fox.

Deforestation in Tasmania.

Saving devils

- One of the greatest threats to devils is a deadly disease that appeared in the 1990s and killed four out of five devils in some areas.
- Luckily there are many people – **conservationists** and **scientists** – working to save Tasmanian Devils, by monitoring the animals and helping to **keep them safe**.
- There are projects that have helped to **breed devils in captivity**, while as a 'safety net' against future disease epidemics a separate population is being established on mainland Australia.

A new population of devils is being established on mainland Australia at Barrington Tops, New South Wales.

First published in 2025 by
New Holland Publishers

newhollandpublishers.com

A record of this book is held at the National Library of Australia.

ISBN 9781760798055

OTHER TITLES IN THE 'DID YOU KNOW?' SERIES:

Capybara
ISBN 9781760798048

Dolphins
ISBN 9781921078000

Kangaroos
ISBN 9781921073861

Koala
ISBN 9781921073878

Lizards
ISBN 9781921073885

Meerkat
ISBN 9781921073892

Penguins
ISBN 9781921073908

Red Panda
ISBN 9781921073915

Sharks
ISBN 9781921078017

For details of these books and hundreds of other Natural History titles see newhollandpublishers.com